Spanish

Grade **2**

Ages 7-8

ball
bola

dolphin
delfín

agua
water

Brighter Child®
an imprint of Carson Dellosa Education

Pronunciation Key

Use the pronunciation key below to learn how to say and make the sound of each Spanish letter.

Spanish Letter	English Pronunciation of Letter	The Sound the Letter Makes	Example of the Letter Sound
a	ah	ah	p<u>o</u>t
b	be	b	<u>b</u>at
c	say	k or s	<u>c</u>at, <u>c</u>ity
d	de	d	<u>d</u>og
e	eh	e	p<u>e</u>t
f	efe	f, ph	<u>f</u>oot
g	hey	g, h	<u>g</u>o, <u>h</u>and
h	ache	silent	silent
i	ee	ee	f<u>ee</u>t
j	hota	h	<u>h</u>ot
k	ka	k	ca<u>k</u>e
l	ele	l	<u>l</u>emon
m	eme	m	<u>m</u>ind
n	ene	n	<u>n</u>o
ñ	eñe	ñ	o<u>ni</u>on
o	o	o	b<u>oa</u>t
p	pe	p	<u>p</u>ot
q	ku	ku	<u>c</u>ool
r	ere	r	<u>r</u>obe
s	ese	s	<u>s</u>o
t	te	t	<u>t</u>oe
u	oo	oo	p<u>oo</u>l
v	ve	v	<u>v</u>ine
w	doblay-oo	w	<u>w</u>e
x	equis	ks	e<u>x</u>it
y	ee griega	y	<u>y</u>ellow
z	seta	s	s<u>u</u>it

Note: The letters "t" and "d" are pronounced with the tongue slightly between the teeth and not behind the teeth.

Brighter Child®
An imprint of Carson Dellosa Education
P.O. Box 35665
Greensboro, NC 27425 USA

ISBN 978-1-4838-1656-2

11-133197784

Table of Contents

Numbers 0–10 4
Numbers 0–10 5
Dot–to–Dot. 6
Numbers 0–20 7
Show Your Numbers 8
Sunshine 0–20. 9
Number Puzzle. 10
Counting On 11
The Alphabet. 12
Using You 13
Picking Pronouns. 14
More Than One. 15
More and More. 16
First Sentences. 17
Action Words. 18
Capitals 19
Categories. 20
Polite Words. 21
Introductions 22
Puzzle of the Week 23
Spanish Months 24
Pictures to Color 25
Rainbow Colors. 26
Color the Cars. 27
Color Copy 28
Food Meanings 29
Mixed–Up Food 30
Food Words 31
Animals All Around 32
Animal Art 33
Clothing 34
Clothing 35
Remember These? 36
What Belongs? 37
Head to Toe 38

Head and Shoulders. 39
Knees and Toes. 40
Family Word Meanings. 41
Family 42
Family Crossword 43
Listen Well 44
Picture This 45
My Neighborhood 46
Places to Go 47
Place Words. 48
Classroom Things. 49
Classroom Words 50
Listen Carefully 51
Songs and Chants. 52
Songs and Chants. 53
Chants 54
Introductions and Greetings . . 55
Introductions and Greetings . . 56
Introductions and Greetings . . 57
Introductions and Greetings . . 58
Introductions and Greetings . . 59
Introductions and Greetings . . 60
Animals. 61
Animals. 62
Clothing 63
Clothing 64
Clothing 65
Clothing 66
Community 67
Community 68
Classroom Objects 69
Classroom Objects 70
Classroom Objects 71
Classroom Objects 72
Answer Key 73–80

Numbers 0–10

Trace, then write each of the number words from 0 to 10 in Spanish. Use the words at the left to help you.

0 cero   cero

1 uno   uno

2 dos   dos

3 tres   tres

4 cuatro   cuatro

5 cinco   cinco

6 seis   seis

7 siete   siete

8 ocho   ocho

9 nueve   nueve

10 diez   diez

Numbers 0–10

Say each word out loud. Circle the number that tells the meaning of the word.

seis	5	0	6
ocho	1	9	8
uno	3	1	8
cero	8	10	0
siete	9	7	1
tres	0	3	5
diez	10	8	7
nueve	4	2	9
cuatro	7	5	4
dos	2	6	3
cinco	6	4	5

Dot-to-Dot

Connect the dots. Start with the Spanish word for one and stop at ten. What shape did you get? _____

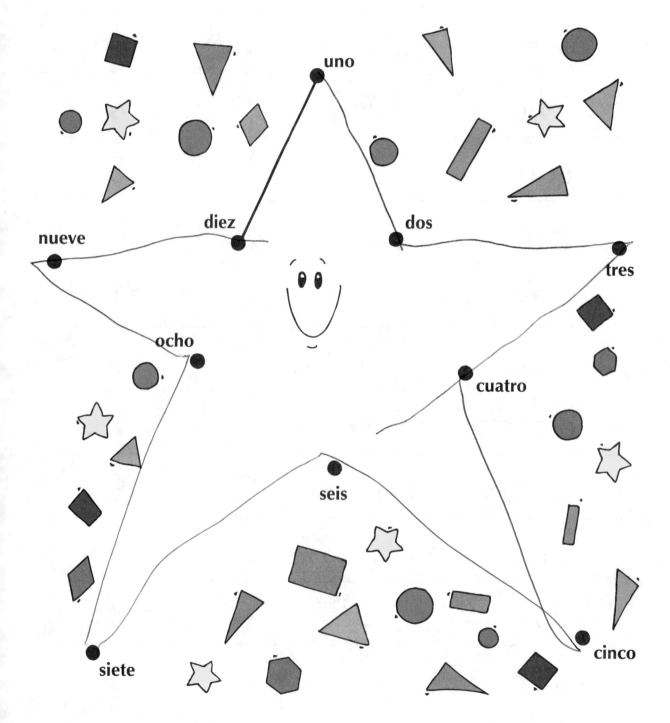

Numbers 0–20

In the left column, write the number words from 0 to 10 in Spanish. Use the words in the box below to help you. Then, in the second column, write the numbers beside each Spanish word. Examples are done for you.

0 cero

1 uno

2 dos

3 tres

4 cuatro

5 cinco

6 seis

7 siete

8 ocho

9 nueve

10 diez

11 once

12 doce

13 trece

14 catorce

15 quince

16 dieciséis

17 diecisiete

18 dieciocho

19 diecinueve

20 veinte

| siete | ocho | uno | seis | nueve | tres |
| cero | cinco | dos | cuatro | diez | |

Now, count from 1 to 20 in Spanish. Point to the numbers as you say them.

Show Your Numbers

In each box, write the number for the word written. Then, draw and color pictures that show the numbers.

dieciséis means 16	**trece** means 3	**ocho** means 8
catorce means 14	**seis** means 6	**once** means 11
dos means 2	**veinte** means 20	**cinco** means 5
doce means 12	**diez** means 10	**quince** means 15

Name **Emma D**

Sunshine 0-20

Write the number for each Spanish word. Cross out the correct number of suns to show the number written in Spanish. The first is done for you.

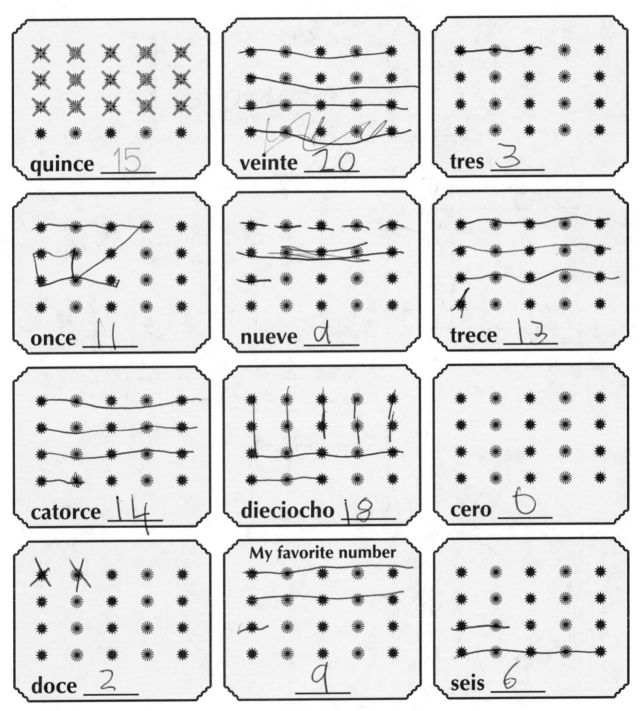

quince _15_

veinte _20_

tres _3_

once _11_

nueve _d_

trece _13_

catorce _14_

dieciocho _18_

cero _0_

doce _2_

My favorite number
_9_

seis _6_

Number Puzzle

Write the English number words in the puzzle spaces. Follow the Spanish clues.

Word Bank

one	eight	eleven	seventeen
two	nine	thirteen	eighteen
six	ten	fourteen	twenty

Down
1. diecisiete
2. veinte
4. uno
8. nueve
9. dieciocho
10. diez

Across
1. seis
3. ocho
5. catorce
6. trece
7. once
10. dos

Counting On

Follow a pattern to write the numbers from 21–29. Change *veinte* (20) to *veinti* and add the number words from *uno* to *nueve*. (Watch for accent marks on *dos*, *tres*, and *seis*.)

Rewrite the number words in the Word Bank in order.

Word Bank

veintiséis	veinticinco	treinta	veintiocho
veintidós	veintiuno	veintinueve	veinticua-
veintisiete	veintitrés		tro

21 _____   26 _____

22 _____   27 _____

23 _____   28 _____

24 _____   29 _____

25 _____   30 _____

Complete the pattern to write the numbers from 31–39. Use the word *y* to join *treinta* (30) with the number words *uno* to *nueve*.

30 _____   35 _____

31 _____   36 _____

32 _____   37 _____

33 _____   38 _____

34 _____   39 _____

The Alphabet

Say the Spanish alphabet out loud. Find the letter that does not appear in the English alphabet.

El abecedario (the alphabet)

a	a	**k**	ka	**t**	te
b	be	**l**	ele	**u**	u
c	ce	**m**	eme	**v**	ve
d	de	**n**	ene	**w**	doble ve
e	e	**ñ**	eñe	**x**	equis
f	efe	**o**	o	**y**	i griega
g	ge	**p**	pe	**z**	zeta
h	hache	**q**	cu		
i	i	**r**	ere		
j	jota	**s**	ese		

Listening Practice

Write the Spanish word for each number below. Then, say each word out loud.

1 _____   5 _____   9 _____   13 _____

2 _____   6 _____   10 _____   14 _____

3 _____   7 _____   11 _____   15 _____

4 _____   8 _____   12 _____   16 _____

Using You

Spanish uses two different forms of the pronoun you.

Tú is used when talking to

1. someone you refer to by a first name.
2. your sister, brother, or cousin.
3. a classmate.
4. a close friend.
5. a child younger than yourself.

tú

Usted (**Ud.**) is used when talking to

1. someone with a title.
2. an older person.
3. a stranger.
4. a person of authority.

usted

Write the names of 6 or more people in each box below.

Use **tú** when you are talking to . . .	Use **usted** when you are talking to . . .

Picking Pronouns

Spanish uses two different forms of the pronoun you.

Tú is used when talking to

1. someone you refer to by a first name.
2. your sister, brother, or cousin.
3. a classmate.
4. a close friend.
5. a child younger than yourself.

tú

Usted (Ud.) is used when talking to

1. someone with a title.
2. an older person.
3. a stranger.
4. a person of authority.

usted

Explain to whom you might be talking and what you are asking in each question.

¿Cómo te llamas tú? _____

¿Cómo se llama usted? _____

¿Cómo estás tú? _____

¿Cómo está usted? _____

¿Cuántos años tienes tú? _____

¿Cuántos años tiene usted? _____

More Than One

Spanish nouns can be placed into two groups—singular nouns (one of something) or plural nouns (more than one of something). Nouns that end in -s are usually plural. Nouns ending in other letters are usually singular.

Read the following familiar nouns. Write **S** if the noun is singular and **P** if the noun is plural.

_____ 1. calcetines   _____ 2. dedo   _____ 3. botas

_____ 4. cuerpo   _____ 5. vegetales _____ 6. ciudad

_____ 7. escuela   _____ 8. sandalias _____ 9. zapatos

_____ 10. guantes   _____ 11. casa   _____ 12. boca

Follow these rules to write the following Spanish words in the plural.

1. If the word ends in a vowel, add -s.

2. If the word ends in a consonant, add -es.

3. If the word ends in z, change the z to c before adding -es.

1. carne _____   6. nariz _____

2. silla _____   7. abrigo _____

3. ciudad _____   8. señor _____

4. lápiz _____   9. borrador _____

5. azul _____   10. pollo _____

15 *Spanish: Grade 2*

More and More

Write the plural form of each Spanish clue word in the puzzle.

Across

1. hombro
4. falda
5. zapato
7. museo
8. nariz
10. gato
11. sombrero
13. oso
14. lápiz

Down

2. borrador
3. vaso
6. escuela
9. casa
12. mesa

First Sentences

Create original sentences in Spanish using these sentence starters and the verbs in the Word Bank. You may use one sentence starter more than once. Write the English meanings on the lines below the Spanish.

Word Bank

comer	beber	dormir	tocar
hablar	limpiar	mirar	dar

Sentence Starters

Me gusta _____ .   (I like _____ .)

No me gusta _____ .   (I don't like _____ .)

Quiero _____ .   (I want _____ .)

Necesito _____ .   (I need _____ .)

1. _____

   _____

2. _____

   _____

3. _____

   _____

4. _____

   _____

5. _____

   _____

Action Words

Refer to the Word Bank to write the Spanish word that matches each picture.

Word Bank	comer	estudiar	limpiar	mirar	jugar	dar
	hablar	beber	dormir	trabajar	tocar	ir

to clean

to touch

to eat

to speak _hablar_

to watch

to drink

to give

to sleep

to study

to go

to work

to play

Capitals

Spanish uses capital letters less often than the English language. Follow these rules as your guide.

Capitalization Rules

1. All Spanish sentences begin with capital letters.

2. Names of people begin with capital letters.

3. Names of places (cities, regions, countries, continents) and holidays begin with capital letters.

4. Titles are not capitalized unless abbreviated (*señor–Sr., usted–Ud.*).

5. Some words that are normally capitalized in English may not be capitalized in Spanish (nationalities, religions, languages, months, and days).

Write *sí* if the word should be capitalized. Write *no* if it should remain lowercase.

1. sarah _____

2. inglés _____

3. navidad _____

4. español _____

5. mexicano _____

6. africa _____

7. señor _____

8. enero _____

9. domingo _____

10. católico _____

11. santa fé _____

12. viernes _____

13. méxico _____

14. julio _____

15. colorado _____

16. miguel _____

Categories

Read the list of words given. Write the words in the proper columns. If the word needs a capital letter, write it that way.

los angeles   españa   ustedes   americano   lunes
maría   susana   san antonio   américa del norte   méxico
uds.   sr.   santa fé   español   católico
inglés   sra.   oceano pacífico   señora   señor
san diego   viernes   juan   josé
señorita   cuba   septiembre   mexicano

People	Places	Titles	Not Capitalized

Polite Words

Say each Spanish expression out loud.

¿Cuántos años tienes?		How old are you?
Tengo seis años.		I am six years old
por favor		please
gracias		thank you

amigo		friend	**amiga**	friend

sí	**no**		**amigos**	 friends

¡Hasta luego!	 	See you later!

Introductions

Say each expression out loud. Circle the picture that tells the meaning of each word.

gracias			
Tengo seis años.			
por favor			
amigo			
amigos			
¡Hasta luego!			
amiga			
sí			

22

Puzzle of the Week

Write the Spanish words in the puzzle.

Across
2. Thursday
7. Wednesday

Down
1. Monday
3. Saturday
4. Friday
5. Sunday
6. Tuesday

Word Bank
jueves	domingo	martes
sábado	viernes	lunes
	miércoles	

Spanish Months

Write the Spanish word for the clue words in the crossword puzzle.

Across

4. July
9. May
10. September
11. June
12. January

Down

1. April
2. November
3. December
5. March
6. February
7. August
8. October

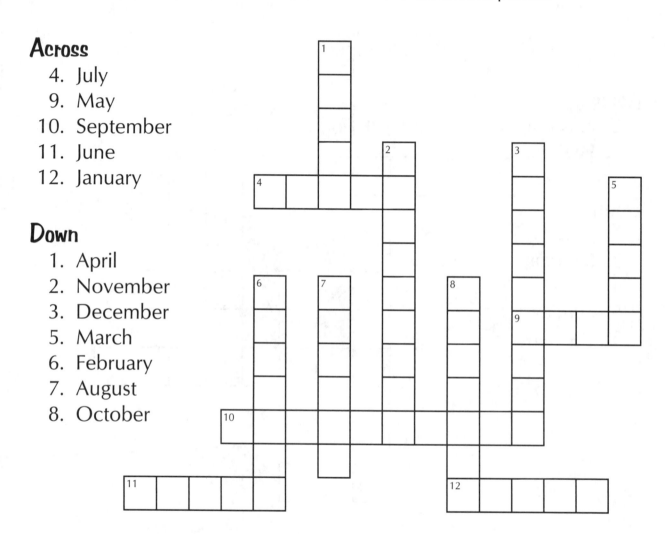

Word Bank

marzo	mayo	diciembre	junio
septiembre	octubre	julio	agosto
abril	enero	febrero	noviembre

Pictures to Color

Color the pictures according to each color word.

rojo

azul

verde

anaranjado

morado

amarillo

Rainbow Colors

Color the picture according to the color words shown.

Color the Cars

Color the cars according to the color words shown.

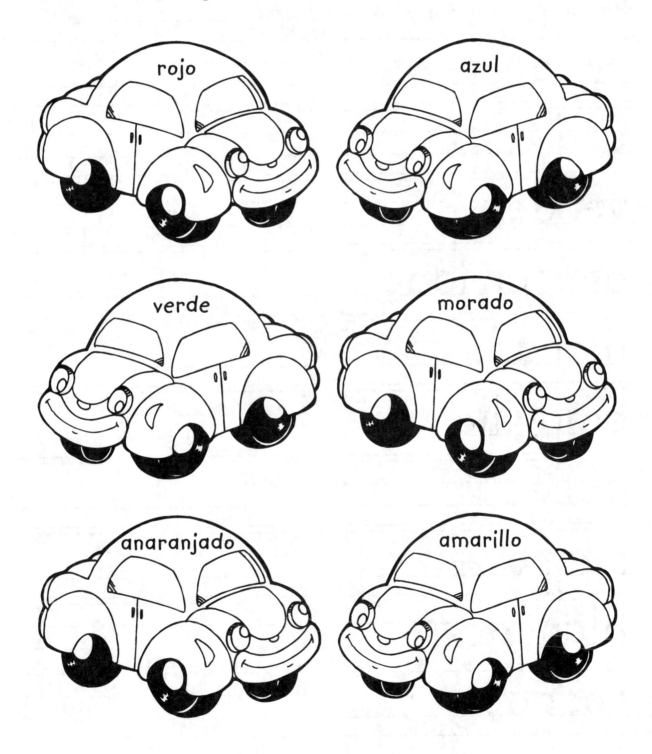

rojo

azul

verde

morado

anaranjado

amarillo

Spanish: Grade 2

Color Copy

Copy the following words in the color of each word.
Which word is hard to see with the actual color? _____

rojo

azul

verde

anaranjado

morado

amarillo

café

negro

blanco

rosado

Food Meanings

Say each word out loud. Circle the picture that shows the meaning of each word.

papa		
ensalada		
queso		
pan		
leche		
pollo		
jugo		

Mixed-Up Food

Draw a line from the word to the food picture.

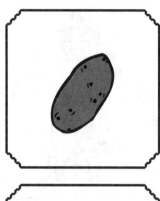

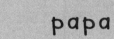
papa

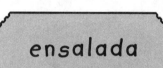
ensalada

queso

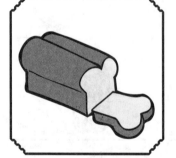

pan

leche

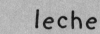
jugo

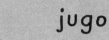
pollo

Food Words

Say each word out loud. Copy each word and color the picture.

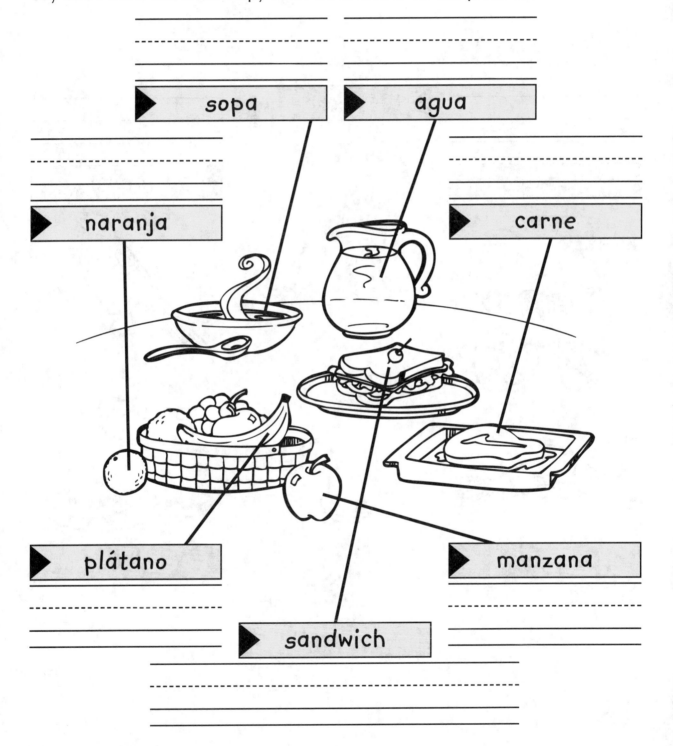

▶ sopa

▶ agua

▶ naranja

▶ carne

▶ plátano

▶ manzana

▶ sandwich

Name _____

Animals All Around

Copy each word and color the pictures.

perro

gato

pájaro

pez

pato

culebra

Animal Art

Choose four animals and draw each animal in its home. Label it with the Spanish animal word.

Clothing

Say each word out loud. Copy each word and color the picture.

pantalones

gorro

vestido

camisa

zapatos

calcetines

Clothing

Say each word out loud. Copy each word and color the picture.

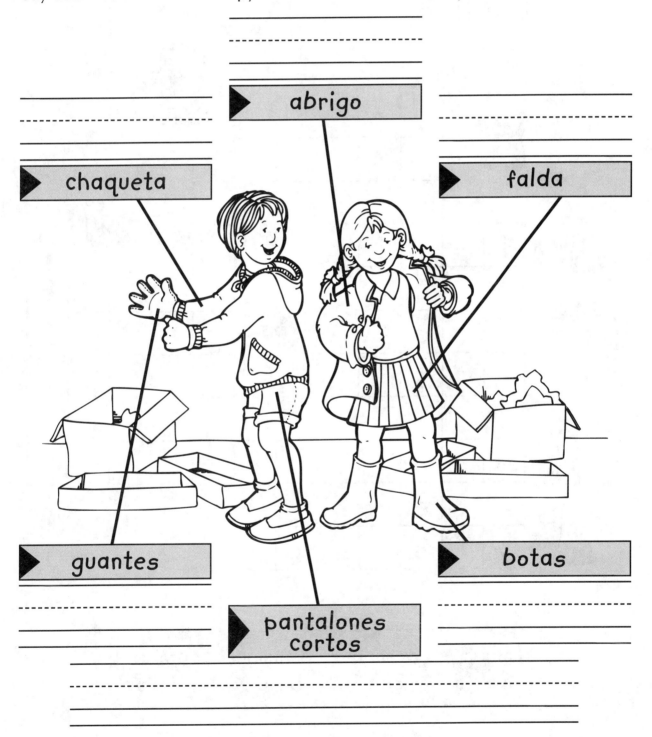

► abrigo

► chaqueta

► falda

► guantes

► botas

► pantalones cortos

Remember These?

Fill in the blanks with the missing letters. Use the Spanish clothing words at the bottom to help you.

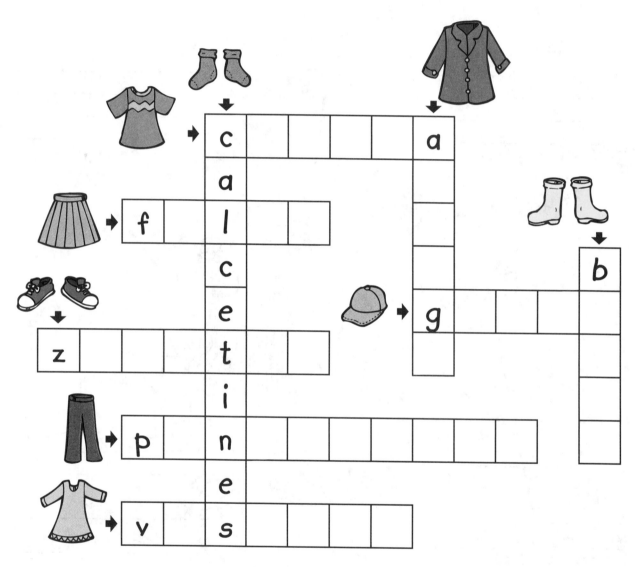

| camisa | vestido | pantalones | falsa |
| zapatos | gorro | abrigo | botas |

What Belongs?

Circle the item that does not belong with the other two. Write its name in Spanish below its picture.

Circle the two items that are alike. Say the item in Spanish that is not like the other two. Color the pictures.

© Carson Dellosa **37** *Spanish: Grade 2*

Name _____

Head to Toe

Using the Word Banks, label the parts of the face and body.

Word Bank

cara   ojos   boca   nariz   dientes   orejas   pelo

Word Bank

cuerpo   cabeza   mano   pierna   hombro
brazo   dedo   pie   rodilla   estómago

Head and Shoulders

Refer to the Word Bank to label each body part in Spanish.

Word Bank

cuerpo	pie
brazo	pierna
cabeza	rodilla
dedo	hombro
mano	estómago

Knees and Toes

Write the Spanish words for the clues in the crossword puzzle.

Word Bank

cuerpo	cabeza	mano	pierna	hombro
brazo	dedo	pie	rodilla	estómago

Across

2. foot
3. body
5. knee
6. head
7. shoulder
9. hand

Down

1. finger or toe
2. leg
4. stomach
8. arm

Family Word Meanings

Say each word out loud. Circle the picture that shows the meaning of each word.

| padre |  |  |

| chica |  | |

| abuela |  | |

| madre |  | |

| abuelo | |  |

| chico | |  |

Spanish: Grade 2

Family

Copy each word and color the pictures.

_____

► madre

_____

► padre

_____

► abuelo

_____

► abuela

_____

► chica

_____

► chico

Let's learn two new words:

_____

► hermano

_____

► hermana

Family Crossword

Use the Spanish words at the bottom of the page to fill in your answers.

Across

1. sister
4. father
5. mother
6. girl
7. boy

Down

1. brother
2. grandmother
3. grandfather

padre	madre
chico	chica
abuelo	abuela
hermano	hermana

Spanish: Grade 2

Listen Well

Say each word out loud. Circle the picture for each Spanish word.

padre			
abuelo			
hermana			
chica			
abuela			
madre			
hermano			
chico			

Picture This

Say each word out loud. Circle the picture that shows the meaning of each word.

| casa |  |  |

| escuela |  |  |

| tienda |  |  |

| parque |  |  |

| biblioteca |  |  |

| museo |  |  |

My Neighborhood

Draw a picture of an imaginary neighborhood. Add streets, trees, and whatever else you wish to make your neighborhood look nice. Color your picture.

Mi barrio

Label your neighborhood with the words you learned.

casa   parque   biblioteca   tienda   escuela   museo

Places to Go

Say each word out loud. Copy each word and color the picture.

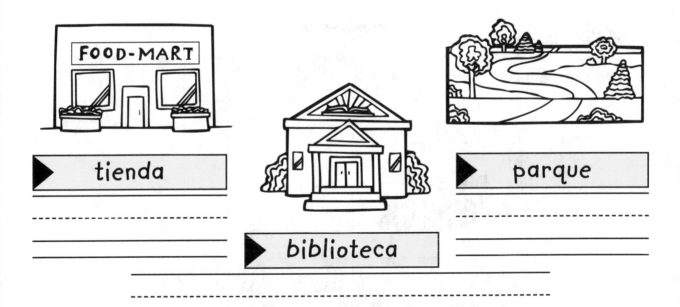

▶ museo

▶ escuela

▶ casa

▶ tienda

FOOD-MART

▶ biblioteca

▶ parque

Place Words

Fill in the blanks for place words. Use the Spanish words at the bottom to help you.

escuela   museo   casa
biblioteca   tienda   parque

Classroom Things

Copy each word and color the picture.

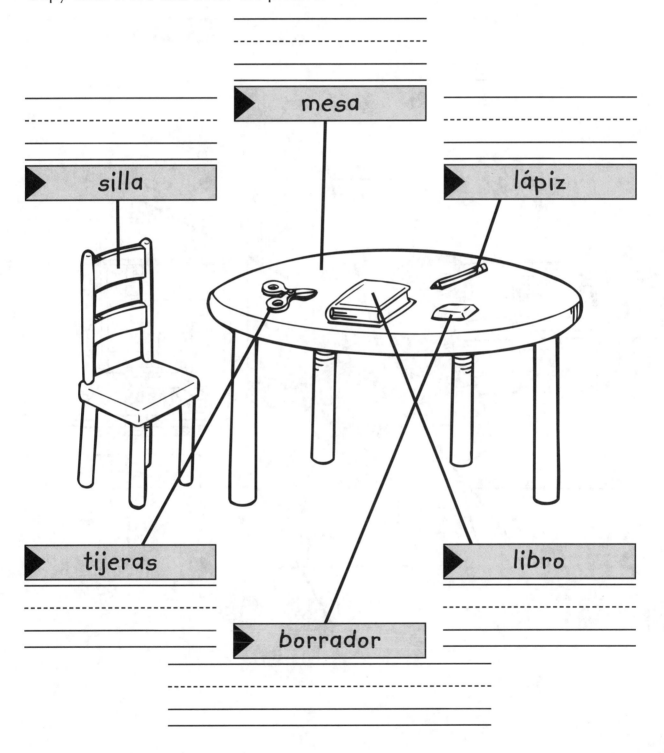

mesa

silla

lápiz

tijeras

borrador

libro

49

Classroom Words

Say each word out loud. Copy each word and color the picture.

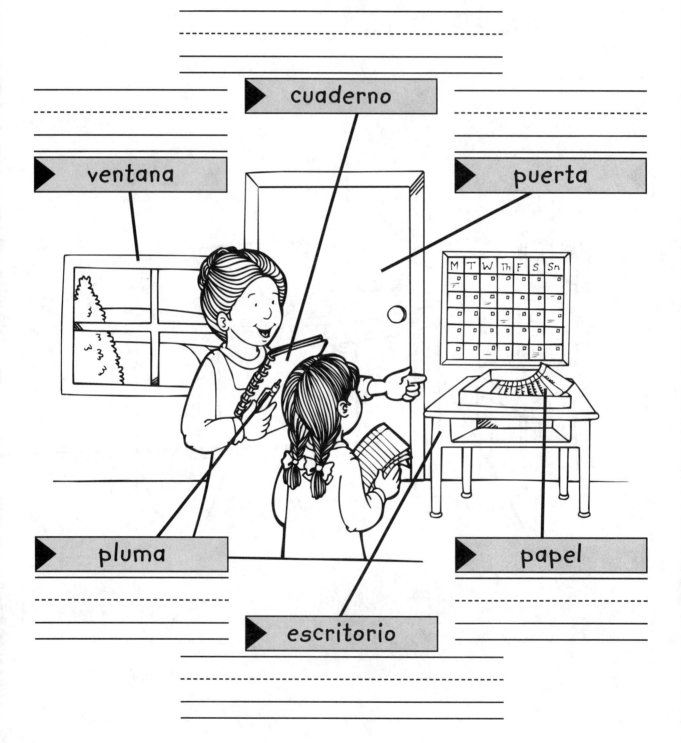

cuaderno

ventana

puerta

pluma

papel

escritorio

Listen Carefully

Say each word out loud. Circle the picture that tells the meaning of each word.

libro			
tijeras			
ventana			
silla			
pluma			
lápiz			
cuaderno			
mesa			
puerta			

Spanish: Grade 2

Songs and Chants

Diez (veinte) amigos
(to the tune of "Ten Little Fingers")

Uno, dos, tres amigos,
cuatro, cinco, seis amigos,
siete, ocho, nueve amigos,
diez amigos son.

Diez, nueve, ocho amigos
siete, seis, cinco amigos
cuatro, tres, dos amigos,
un amigo es.

Once, doce, trece amigos,
catorce, quince, dieciséis amigos,
diecisiete, dieciocho,
diecinueve amigos,
veinte amigos son.

Community Song
(to the tune of "Here We Go 'Round the Mulberry Bush")

Escuela is school,
museo — museum,
casa is house,
tienda is store,
biblioteca is library,
parque is the park for me!

Songs and Chants

Family Song
(to the tune of "Are You Sleeping?")

Padre — father,
madre — mother,
chico — boy,
chica — girl,
abuelo is grandpa,
abuela is grandma.
Our family, our family.

Hermano — brother,
hermana — sister,
chico — boy,
chica — girl,
padre y madre,
abuelo y abuela.
Our family, our family.

Los días de la semana
(to the tune of "Clementine")

Domingo, lunes,
martes, miércoles,
jueves, viernes, sábado,
domingo, lunes,
martes, miércoles,
jueves, viernes, sábado. (Repitan)

53 *Spanish: Grade 2*

Chants

Body Chant

Cabeza, hombros, rodillas, dedos, rodillas, dedos, rodillas, dedos
Cabeza, hombros, rodillas, dedos
Ojos, orejas, boca, nariz.

Number Chant

Dos y dos son cuatro, cuatro y dos son seis, seis y dos son ocho, y ocho más, dieciséis.
(Two and two are four, four and two are six, six and two are eight, and eight more, sixteen.)

Clothing Chant

Abrigo rosado, vestido blanco,
camisa café, sombrero morado,
blusas verdes, pantalones rojos,
botas azules, zapatos negros.

Pink coat, white dress,
brown shirt, purple hat,
green blouses, red pants,
blue boots, black shoes.

Adjective Chant

La casa es grande, la mesa—pequeña,
la puerta—cerrada, la ventana abierta.

The house is big, the table—small,
the door—closed, the window—open.

Papa Chant

Yo como una papa, no como a mi papá.
    I eat a potato, I don't eat my dad.
Una papa es comida, un papá es un padre.
    A papa is a potato, a papá is a father.

*Due to differences in languages, literal translations of chants may lose meaning and/or the sense of rhythm.

Introductions and Greetings

Cut out the learning cards. Practice saying the Spanish words using the learning cards.

¡Hola!

¿Cómo te llamas?

Me llamo _____.

¡Adiós!

¿Cómo estás?

bien

This page is intentionally left blank.

Introductions and Greetings

Cut out the learning cards. Practice saying the Spanish words using the learning cards.

mal

así, así

¿Cuántos años tienes?

Tengo _____ años.

sí

no

This page is intentionally left blank.

Introductions and Greetings

Cut out the learning cards. Practice saying the Spanish words using the learning cards.

This page is intentionally left blank.

Animals

Cut out the learning cards. Practice saying the Spanish words using the
learning cards.

gato

perro

pájaro

pez

pato

culebra

This page is intentionally left blank.

Clothing

Cut out the learning cards. Practice saying the Spanish words using the learning cards.

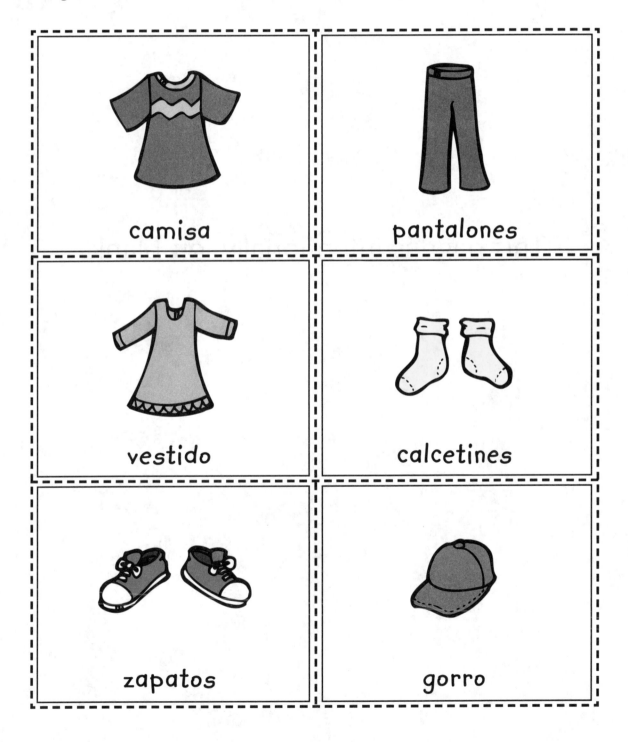

camisa

pantalones

vestido

calcetines

zapatos

gorro

This page is intentionally left blank.

Name _____

Clothing

Cut out the learning cards. Practice saying the Spanish words using the learning cards.

chaqueta

pantalones cortos

botas

guantes

falda

abrigo

65

This page is intentionally left blank.

Community

Cut out the learning cards. Practice saying the Spanish words using the learning cards.

escuela

tienda

museo

biblioteca

casa

parque

This page is intentionally left blank.

Classroom Objects

Cut out the learning cards. Practice saying the Spanish words using the learning cards.

silla

mesa

tijeras

libro

lápiz

borrador

This page is intentionally left blank.

Classroom Objects

Cut out the learning cards. Practice saying the Spanish words using the learning cards.

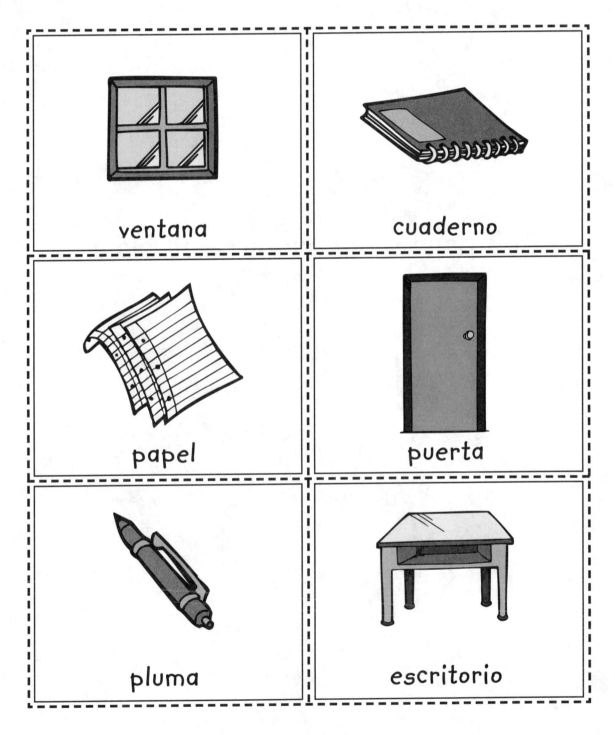

ventana

cuaderno

papel

puerta

pluma

escritorio

This page is intentionally left blank.

Numbers 0–10

Trace, then write each of the number words from 0 to 10 in Spanish. Use the words at the left to help you.

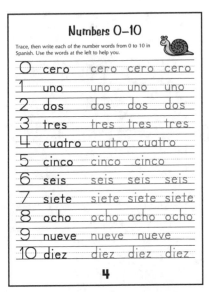

0	cero	cero cero cero
1	uno	uno uno uno
2	dos	dos dos dos
3	tres	tres tres tres
4	cuatro	cuatro cuatro
5	cinco	cinco cinco
6	seis	seis seis seis
7	siete	siete siete siete
8	ocho	ocho ocho ocho
9	nueve	nueve nueve
10	diez	diez diez diez

4

Numbers 0–10

Say each word out loud. Circle the number that tells the meaning of the word.

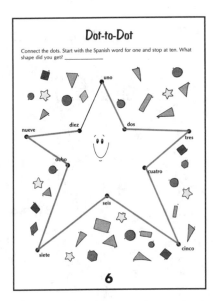

seis	5	0	(6)
ocho	1	9	(8)
uno	3	(1)	8
cero	8	10	(0)
siete	9	(7)	1
tres	0	(3)	5
diez	(10)	8	7
nueve	4	2	(9)
cuatro	7	5	(4)
dos	(2)	6	3
cinco	6	4	(5)

5

Dot-to-Dot

Connect the dots. Start with the Spanish word for one and stop at ten. What shape did you get? _____

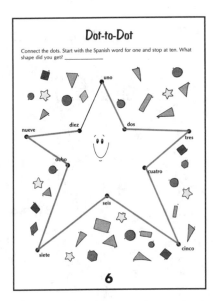

6

Numbers 0–20

In the left column, write the number words from 0 to 10 in Spanish. Use the words in the box below to help you. Then, in the second column, write the numbers beside each Spanish word. Examples are done for you.

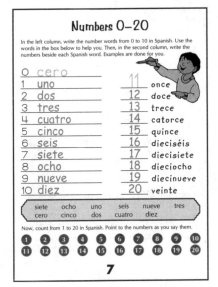

0	cero	11	once
1	uno	12	doce
2	dos	13	trece
3	tres	14	catorce
4	cuatro	15	quince
5	cinco	16	dieciséis
6	seis	17	diecisiete
7	siete	18	dieciocho
8	ocho	19	diecinueve
9	nueve	20	veinte
10	diez		

siete ocho uno seis nueve tres
cero cinco dos cuatro diez

Now, count from 1 to 20 in Spanish. Point to the numbers as you say them.

1 2 3 4 5 6 7 8 9 10
11 12 13 14 15 16 17 18 19 20

7

Show Your Numbers

In each box, write the number for the word written. Then, draw and color pictures that show the numbers.

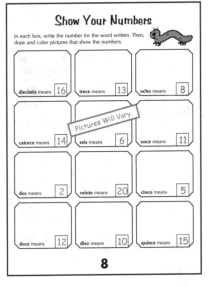

dieciséis means	16	trece means	13	ocho means	8
catorce means	14	seis means	6	once means	11
dos means	2	veinte means	20	cinco means	5
doce means	12	diez means	10	quince means	15

Pictures Will Vary.

8

Sunshine 0–20

Write the number for each Spanish word. Cross out the correct number of suns to show the number written in Spanish. The first is done for you.

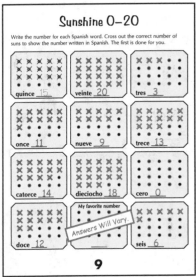

quince	15	veinte	20	tres	3
once	11	nueve	9	trece	13
catorce	14	dieciocho	18	cero	0
doce	12	My favorite number *Answers Will Vary.*		seis	6

9

Spanish: Grade 2

Number Puzzle

Write the English number words in the puzzle spaces. Follow the Spanish clues.

Word Bank

one	eight	eleven	seventeen
two	nine	thirteen	eighteen
six	ten	fourteen	twenty

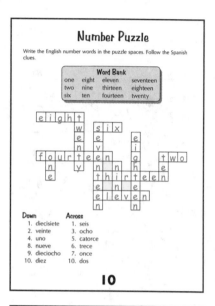

Crossword grid answers:
- eight
- six
- twenty
- fourteen
- nine
- two
- thirteen
- eleven

Down
1. diecisiete
2. veinte
4. uno
8. nueve
9. dieciocho
10. diez

Across
1. seis
3. ocho
5. catorce
6. trece
7. once
10. dos

10

Counting On

Follow a pattern to write the numbers from 21–29. Change *veinte* (20) to *veinti* and add the number words from *uno* to *nueve*. (Watch for accent marks on *dos*, *tres*, and *seis*.)

Rewrite the number words in the Word Bank in order.

Word Bank

veintiséis	veinticinco	treinta	veintiocho
veintidós	veintiuno	veintinueve	veinticuatro
	veintisiete	veintitrés	

21 veintiuno   26 veintiséis
22 veintidós   27 veintisiete
23 veintitrés   28 veintiocho
24 veinticuatro   29 veintinueve
25 veinticinco   30 treinta

Complete the pattern to write the numbers from 31–39. Use the word *y* to join *treinta* (30) with the number words *uno* to *nueve*.

30 treinta   35 treinta y cinco
31 treinta y uno   36 treinta y seis
32 treinta y dos   37 treinta y siete
33 treinta y tres   38 treinta y ocho
34 treinta y cuatro   39 treinta y nueve

11

The Alphabet

Say the Spanish alphabet out loud. Find the letter that does not appear in the English alphabet.

El abecedario (the alphabet)

a	a	k	ka	t	te
b	be	l	ele	u	u
c	ce	m	eme	v	ve
d	de	n	ene	w	doble ve
e	e	ñ	eñe	x	equis
f	efe	o	o	y	i griega
g	ge	p	pe	z	zeta
h	hache	q	cu		
i	i	r	ere		
j	jota	s	ese		

Listening Practice

Write the Spanish word for each number below. Then, say each word out loud.

1 uno   5 cinco   9 nueve   13 trece
2 dos   6 seis   10 diez   14 catorce
3 tres   7 siete   11 once   15 quince
4 cuatro   8 ocho   12 doce   16 dieciséis

12

Using You

Spanish uses two different forms of the pronoun you.

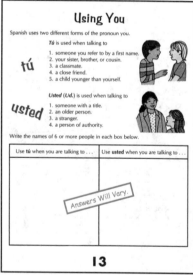

tú

Tú is used when talking to
1. someone you refer to by a first name.
2. your sister, brother, or cousin.
3. a classmate.
4. a close friend.
5. a child younger than yourself.

usted

Usted (Ud.) is used when talking to
1. someone with a title.
2. an older person.
3. a stranger.
4. a person of authority.

Write the names of 6 or more people in each box below.

Use **tú** when you are talking to . . .	Use **usted** when you are talking to . . .
Answers Will Vary.	

13

Picking Pronouns

Spanish uses two different forms of the pronoun you.

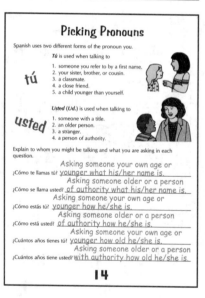

tú

Tú is used when talking to
1. someone you refer to by a first name.
2. your sister, brother, or cousin.
3. a classmate.
4. a close friend.
5. a child younger than yourself.

usted

Usted (Ud.) is used when talking to
1. someone with a title.
2. an older person.
3. a stranger.
4. a person of authority.

Explain to whom you might be talking and what you are asking in each question.

¿Cómo te llamas tú? Asking someone your own age or younger what his/her name is.
¿Cómo se llama usted? Asking someone older or a person of authority what his/her name is.
¿Cómo estás tú? Asking someone your own age or younger how he/she is.
¿Cómo está usted? Asking someone older or a person of authority how he/she is.
¿Cuántos años tienes tú? Asking someone your own age or younger how old he/she is.
¿Cuántos años tiene usted? Asking someone older or a person with authority how old he/she is.

14

More Than One

Spanish nouns can be placed into two groups—singular nouns (one of something) or plural nouns (more than one of something). Nouns that end in –s are usually plural. Nouns ending in other letters are usually singular.

Read the following familiar nouns. Write **S** if the noun is singular and **P** if the noun is plural.

P 1. calcetines   S 2. dedo   P 3. botas
S 4. cuerpo   P 5. vegetales   S 6. ciudad
S 7. escuela   P 8. sandalias   P 9. zapatos
P 10. guantes   S 11. casa   S 12. boca

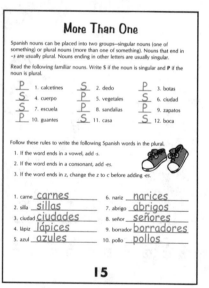

Follow these rules to write the following Spanish words in the plural.

1. If the word ends in a vowel, add -s.
2. If the word ends in a consonant, add -es.
3. If the word ends in z, change the z to c before adding -es.

1. carne carnes   6. nariz narices
2. silla sillas   7. abrigo abrigos
3. ciudad ciudades   8. señor señores
4. lápiz lápices   9. borrador borradores
5. azul azules   10. pollo pollos

15

More and More

Write the plural form of each Spanish clue word in the puzzle.

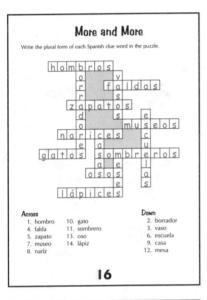

Across
1. hombro
4. falda
5. zapato
7. museo
8. nariz
10. gato
11. sombrero
13. oso
14. lápiz

Down
2. borrador
3. vaso
6. escuela
9. casa
12. mesa

16

First Sentences

Create original sentences in Spanish using these sentence starters and the verbs in the Word Bank. You may use one sentence starter more than once. Write the English meanings on the lines below the Spanish.

Word Bank
comer   beber   dormir   tocar
hablar   limpiar   mirar   dar

Sentence Starters
Me gusta _____ .   (I like _____ .)
No me gusta _____   (I don't like _____ .)
Quiero _____ .   (I want _____ .)
Necesito _____ .   (I need _____ .)

1. _____
2. _____
3. _____
Sentences Will Vary.
4. _____
5. _____

17

Action Words

Refer to the Word Bank to write the Spanish word that matches each picture.

| Word Bank | comer | estudiar | limpiar | mirar | jugar | dar |
| | hablar | beber | dormir | trabajar | tocar | ir |

to clean — limpiar
to touch — tocar
to eat — comer
to speak — hablar
to watch — mirar
to drink — beber
to give — dar
to sleep — dormir
to study — estudiar
to go — ir
to work — trabajar
to play — jugar

18

Capitals

Spanish uses capital letters less often than the English language. Follow these rules as your guide.

Capitalization Rules
1. All Spanish sentences begin with capital letters.
2. Names of people begin with capital letters.
3. Names of places (cities, regions, countries, continents) and holidays begin with capital letters.
4. Titles are not capitalized unless abbreviated (señor–Sr., usted–Ud.).
5. Some words that are normally capitalized in English may not be capitalized in Spanish (nationalities, religions, languages, months, and days).

Write *sí* if the word should be capitalized. Write *no* if it should remain lowercase.

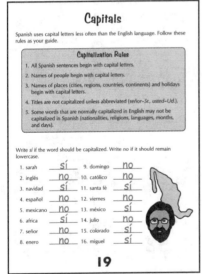

1. sarah — **sí**
2. inglés — **no**
3. navidad — **sí**
4. español — **no**
5. mexicano — **no**
6. africa — **sí**
7. señor — **no**
8. enero — **no**
9. domingo — **no**
10. católico — **no**
11. santa fé — **sí**
12. viernes — **no**
13. méxico — **sí**
14. julio — **no**
15. colorado — **sí**
16. miguel — **sí**

19

Categories

Read the list of words given. Write the words in the proper columns. If the word needs a capital letter, write it that way.

los angeles   españa   ustedes   americano   lunes
maría   susana   san antonio   américa del norte   méxico
uds.   sr.   santa fé   español   católico
inglés   sra.   oceano pacífico   señora   señor
san diego   viernes   juan   josé
señorita   cuba   septiembre   mexicano

People	Places	Titles	Not Capitalized
María	Los Angeles	Uds.	inglés
Susana	San Diego	Sr.	señorita
Juan	España	Sra.	viernes
José	Cuba		ustedes
	San Antonio		septiembre
	Santa Fé		americano
	Océano Pacifico		español
	América del Norte		señora
	México		mexicano
			lunes
			católico
			señor

20

Introductions

Say each expression out loud. Circle the picture that tells the meaning of each word.

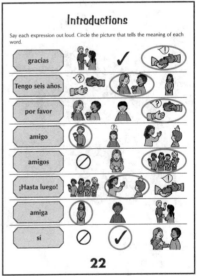

gracias
Tengo seis años.
por favor
amigo
amigos
¡Hasta luego!
amiga
sí

22

Puzzle of the Week

Write the Spanish words in the puzzle.

Across
2. Thursday
7. Wednesday

Down
1. Monday
3. Saturday
4. Friday
5. Sunday
6. Tuesday

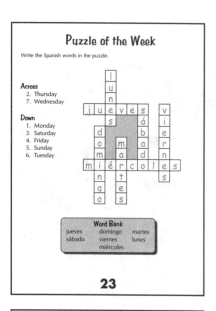

Word Bank

jueves	domingo	martes
sábado	viernes	lunes
miércoles		

23

Spanish Months

Write the Spanish word for the clue words in the crossword puzzle.

Across
4. July
9. May
10. September
11. June
12. January

Down
1. April
2. November
3. December
5. March
6. February
7. August
8. October

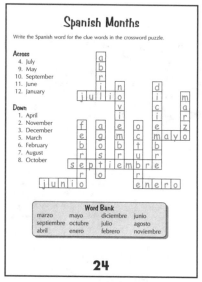

Word Bank

marzo	mayo	diciembre	junio
septiembre	octubre	julio	agosto
abril	enero	febrero	noviembre

24

Pictures to Color

Color the pictures according to each color word.

rojo   azul

verde   anaranjado

morado   amarillo

25

Rainbow Colors

Color the picture according to the color words shown.

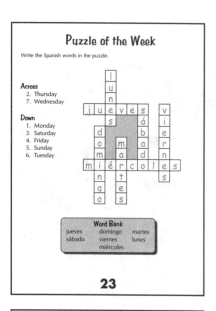

rojo
anaranjado
amarillo
verde
azul
morado

26

Color the Cars

Color the cars according to the color words shown.

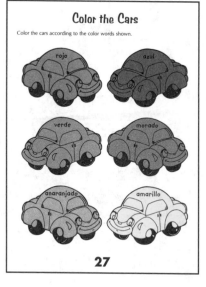

rojo   azul

verde   morado

anaranjado   amarillo

27

Color Copy

Copy the following words in the color of each word.
Which word is hard to see with the actual color? blanco (white)

rojo   rojo
azul   azul
verde   verde
anaranjado   anaranjado
morado   morado
amarillo   amarillo
café   café
negro   negro
blanco   blanco
rosado   rosado

28

Food Meanings

Say each word out loud. Circle the picture that shows the meaning of each word.

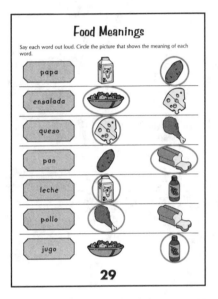

29

Mixed-Up Food

Draw a line from the word to the food picture.

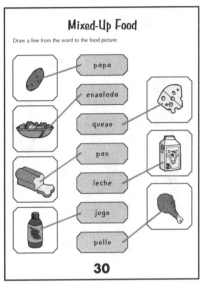

30

Food Words

Say each word out loud. Copy each word and color the picture.

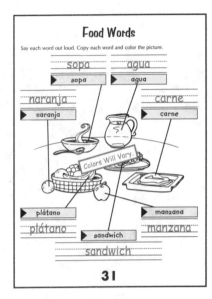

sopa — sopa
agua — agua
naranja — naranja
carne — carne
plátano — plátano
manzana — manzana
sandwich — sandwich

Colors Will Vary.

31

Animals All Around

Copy each word and color the pictures.

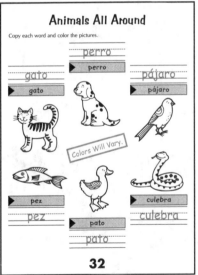

perro — perro
gato — gato
pájaro — pájaro
pez — pez
culebra — culebra
pato — pato

Colors Will Vary.

32

Animal Art

Choose four animals and draw each animal in its home. Label it with the Spanish animal word.

Animals Will Vary.

33

Clothing

Say each word out loud. Copy each word and color the picture.

pantalones — pantalones
gorro — gorro
vestido — vestido
camisa — camisa
calcetines — calcetines
zapatos — zapatos

Colors Will Vary.

34

Spanish: Grade 2

Clothing

Say each word out loud. Copy each word and color the picture.

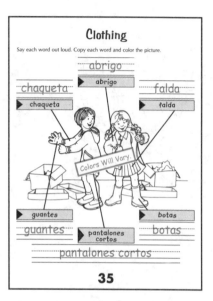

abrigo
abrigo

chaqueta
chaqueta

falda
falda

guantes
guantes

pantalones cortos

pantalones cortos

botas
botas

Colors Will Vary.

35

Remember These?

Fill in the blanks with the missing letters. Use the Spanish clothing words at the bottom to help you.

| camisa | vestido | pantalones | falsa |
| zapatos | gorro | abrigo | botas |

36

What Belongs?

Circle the item that does not belong with the other two. Write its name in Spanish below its picture.

gorro

guantes

pantalones

Circle the two items that are alike. Say the item in Spanish that is not like the other two. Color the pictures.

Colors Will Vary.

37

Head to Toe

Using the Word Banks, label the parts of the face and body.

nariz
ojos
orejas
dientes
pelo
cara
boca

Word Bank
cara   ojos   boca   nariz   dientes   orejas   pelo

mano
hombro
dedo
cuerpo
estómago
brazo
pie
cabeza
rodilla
dedo
pierna

Word Bank
| cuerpo | cabeza | mano | pierna | hombro |
| brazo | dedo | pie | rodilla | estómago |

38

Head and Shoulders

Refer to the Word Bank to label each body part in Spanish.

cabeza
hombro
brazo
cuerpo
estómago
mano
rodilla
dedo
pierna
pie

Word Bank
cuerpo	pie
brazo	pierna
cabeza	rodilla
dedo	hombro
mano	estómago

39

Knees and Toes

Write the Spanish words for the clues in the crossword puzzle.

Word Bank
| cuerpo | cabeza | mano | pierna | hombro |
| brazo | dedo | pie | rodilla | estómago |

Across
2. foot
3. body
5. knee
6. head
7. shoulder
9. hand

Down
1. finger or toe
2. leg
4. stomach
8. arm

40

Family Word Meanings

Say each word out loud. Circle the picture that shows the meaning of each word.

padre		
chica		
abuela		
madre		
abuelo		
chico		

41

Family

Copy each word and color the pictures.

madre
▶ madre

padre
▶ padre

abuelo
▶ abuelo

abuela
▶ abuela

chica
▶ chica

chico
▶ chico

Let's learn two new words. *Colors Will Vary.*

hermano
▶ hermano

hermana
▶ hermana

42

Family Crossword

Use the Spanish words at the bottom of the page to fill in your answers.

				h	e	r	m	a	n	a
p	a	d	r	e			b		u		b
			r				m	a	d	r	e	e
c	h	i	c	a			l		l		u
			n				a		a		l
c	h	i	c	o							o

Across
1. sister
4. father
5. mother
6. girl
7. boy

Down
1. brother
2. grandmother
3. grandfather

padre   madre
chico   chica
abuelo   abuela
hermano hermana

43

Listen Well

Say each word out loud. Circle the picture for each Spanish word.

padre			
abuelo			
hermana			
chica			
abuela			
madre			
hermano			
chico			

44

Picture This

Say each word out loud. Circle the picture that shows the meaning of each word.

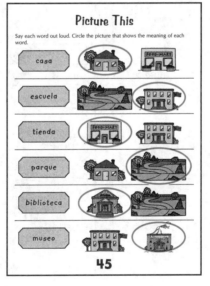

casa		
escuela		
tienda		
parque		
biblioteca		
museo		

45

My Neighborhood

Draw a picture of an imaginary neighborhood. Add streets, trees, and whatever else you wish to make your neighborhood look nice. Color your picture.

Mi barrio

Pictures Will Vary.

Label your neighborhood with the words you learned.

casa   parque   biblioteca   tienda   escuela   museo

46

79

Spanish: Grade 2

Places to Go

Say each word out loud. Copy each word and color the picture.

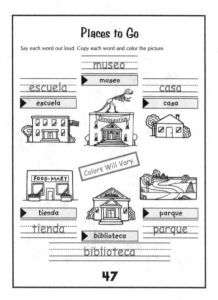

museo
▶ museo

escuela
▶ escuela

casa
▶ casa

Colors Will Vary.

tienda
▶ tienda

parque
▶ parque

biblioteca
▶ biblioteca

47

Place Words

Fill in the blanks for place words. Use the Spanish words at the bottom to help you.

| escuela | museo | casa |
| biblioteca | tienda | parque |

48

Classroom Things

Copy each word and color the picture.

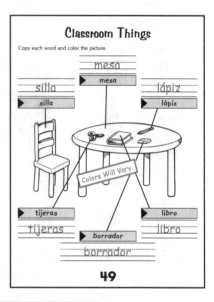

mesa
▶ mesa

silla
▶ silla

lápiz
▶ lápiz

Colors Will Vary.

tijeras
▶ tijeras

libro
▶ libro

borrador
▶ borrador

49

Classroom Words

Say each word out loud. Copy each word and color the picture.

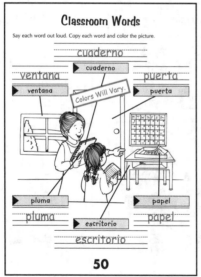

cuaderno
▶ cuaderno

ventana
▶ ventana

puerta
▶ puerta

Colors Will Vary.

pluma
▶ pluma

papel
▶ papel

escritorio
▶ escritorio

50

Listen Carefully

Say each word out loud. Circle the picture that tells the meaning of each word.

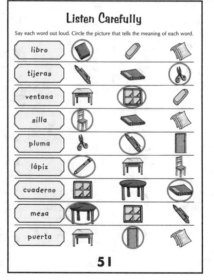

libro

tijeras

ventana

silla

pluma

lápiz

cuaderno

mesa

puerta

51